THIS BOOK IS A GIFT OF:
FRIENDS OF THE ORINDA LIBRARY

CONTRA COSTA COUNTY LIBRARY

George H.W. Bush

History Maker Bios

Catherine A. Welch

LERN   • MINNEAPOLIS

To my wonderful sons, John and Michael, who love history and politics and taught each other about friendship

The author thanks Judith Stark, Jackie Hoffman, and the staff of the Southbury Public Library in Connecticut for help in gathering material for this book.

Illustrations by Tad Butler

Text copyright © 2008 by Catherine A. Welch
Illustrations copyright © 2008 by Lerner Publishing Group, Inc.

Lerner Publications Company
A division of Lerner Publishing Group, Inc.
241 First Avenue North
Minneapolis, MN 55401 U.S.A.

Website address: www.lernerbooks.com

Library of Congress Cataloging-in-Publication Data

Welch, Catherine A.
    George H.W. Bush / by Catherine A. Welch.
      p.   cm. — (History maker biographies)
    Includes bibliographical references and index.
    ISBN 978–0–8225–8895–5 (lib. bdg. : alk. paper)
    1. Bush, George, 1924—Juvenile literature. 2. Presidents—United States—
Biography—Juvenile literature. I. Title.
    E882.W45 2008
    973.928092—dc22 [B]   2007040142

Manufactured in the United States of America
1 2 3 4 5 6 – PA – 13 12 11 10 09 08

Table of Contents

INTRODUCTION

George Herbert Walker Bush was born on June 12, 1924. At that time, the United States was not yet such a powerful country. But by World War II (1939–1945), it was becoming a mighty force in world affairs.

George lived most of his life touched by war. He fought in World War II. He became a national leader during the Cold War. And when the United States began facing new threats, George became president.

This is his story.

1 FROM BOY TO PILOT

George H. W. Bush learned about friendship from his three brothers and one sister. They grew up in Greenwich, Connecticut, in a house with eight bedrooms. George and his older brother, Prescott Jr., loved spending time together. They always shared a bedroom. Sometimes they played baseball there, batting around their dad's rolled up socks.

Their father, Prescott, was a successful businessman. But the boys were often afraid of him. Prescott was strict and formal. He even made his sons wear jackets and ties to dinner.

George was more like their mother, Dorothy. She was cheerful and a great tennis player. She was the fastest runner on her baseball team. But she never bragged, and she taught George not to brag about his talents. Dorothy had strict rules about how to treat others. Be a team player, she told George. Be a good sport and don't complain. Be honest and help others.

In this picture, George (RIGHT) is four years old. His sister, Nancy (LEFT), is two years old. George's brothers Jonathan and William "Bucky" came later.

George loved his family and had a carefree childhood. The Bushes had money for a cook, two maids, a chauffeur (driver), and private schools. George attended Greenwich Country Day School. Later, he went to Phillips Academy in Andover, Massachusetts.

In the summers, George and his family visited his Grandfather Walker at his house in Maine. George learned how to fish and handle a lobster boat.

GEORGE'S FAMILY ROOTS

George's father and mother came from English families. Early Bushes may have arrived on the *Mayflower*. The Walkers, the family of George's mother, settled in Maine in the 1600s. George is a distant cousin of Elizabeth II, queen of England. He is related to fifteen American presidents, including Washington and Lincoln. George was raised in the Episcopal faith. It has its roots in Great Britain.

Japanese fighter planes bombed the U.S.S. SHAW in Pearl Harbor.

In 1941, when George was seventeen, his world suddenly changed. On December 7, Japan attacked the United States at Pearl Harbor, a naval base in Hawaii. The Japanese attack forced the United States into World War II.

While at home for Christmas, George thought about the war. He wondered what he should do after graduation. He also went to a dance. There, he met sixteen-year-old Barbara Pierce, a lively talker.

When George returned to Andover, he and Barbara wrote letters to each other. George also thought about joining the U.S. Navy. He was accepted at Yale University for the next year. But he wanted to become a navy pilot. George's father cried when he heard the news. He knew George could be killed in the war.

George was nervous when he began navy training. Some cadets were fearless and learned to fly quickly. But George had to face his fears and work hard. For one thing, he was left-handed. Controls were set up for right-handed pilots.

By early 1944, George had finished training. He joined others on the aircraft carrier *San Jacinto* in the Pacific Ocean. Planes took off from this ship to attack nearby Japanese islands. Takeoffs and landings on the ship's deck were dangerous. Pilots could crash their planes into the sea or deck. George saw men die in horrible accidents.

The U.S.S. SAN JACINTO could travel quickly. It carried fighter planes to places that larger carriers could not reach.

On September 2, 1944, George flew on a special bombing mission. The target was a Japanese radio station on the island of Chichi-Jima. His two crewmen were William "Ted" White and John Delaney.

As George flew to the island, Japanese gunfire hit their plane. Flames flashed along the wings. George knew the plane was about to crash. But he pushed his fears aside. He reached the target and dropped his bombs.

Then he headed back over the water and cried out to his crewmen. Bail out! Moments later, George jumped from the plane himself. He searched for the two men. But he never found them.

George makes notes in the cockpit of his plane.

The crew of the submarine U.S.S. FINBACK rescues George from the ocean.

George floated alone in a raft, praying the Japanese would not capture him. Finally, a U.S. submarine rose from the water. He was rescued!

George was sad to learn that Ted and John had died. He often wondered why his life was spared that day. But he looked forward to seeing his family and Barbara again. Several months later, he made an important visit home—for his wedding!

2 OIL AND POLITICS

On January 6, 1945, George and Barbara married. In August, the Japanese surrendered, ending the war. The couple moved to New Haven, Connecticut. There, George studied at Yale and made many friends. He joined Skull and Bones, a secret club for the brightest or wealthiest Yale men. And his first child, George Walker Bush, was born.

After graduation, George took his family to Texas. Navy buddies had told him about the oil business there. Neil Mallon, a family friend, gave him a job in Odessa.

George put in long hours learning the oil business. He swept out warehouses, painted oil-drilling machines, and worked as a salesman. Along the way, he got help from his Uncle Herbie. Herbie knew wealthy people. They helped George start an oil company with a friend. George's father and Yale friends also helped with money. George became successful in the oil business.

George (LEFT) talks to a worker at an oil field in Texas.

Meanwhile, George and Barbara's second child, Robin, was born. In 1953, Barbara gave birth to John Ellis, called Jeb. Sadly, three-year-old Robin died that year. The family was heartbroken. But by the end of 1959, George and Barbara had three more children—Neil, Marvin, and Dorothy.

By this time, George's father had become a United States senator from Connecticut. George became interested in politics too. He had made a lot of money. He wanted to serve his country as a senator. But would Texas folks vote for him?

Prescott and Dorothy Bush attend a campaign rally. Prescott was elected to the Senate in 1952.

Towers containing oil-drilling machinery line the street in Kilgore, Texas.

For a long time, most Texans voted for Democrats. But George felt he belonged in the Republican Party, like his father.

Luckily for him, Texans were starting to vote for Republicans. Some Texans didn't like the changes Democrats wanted. Some Democrats wanted the government to control certain oil drilling. If this happened, Texas oil companies could lose money.

Some Democrats also wanted to help farmers and laborers. They wanted poor workers, including many African Americans and Mexican Americans, to make more money. But wealthier Texans did not want to pay workers higher wages.

In 1964, George ran for the Senate against a Democrat, Ralph Yarborough. But George lost the election. After the election, George was sorry he had supported some Republican ideas. George really did want to help poor people. He did believe in civil rights for blacks. He thought they should have equal rights. In many parts of the South, blacks were not let into the same schools, restaurants, restrooms, and other public places that whites used.

In 1966, George was elected to the U.S. House of Representatives. As a congressman, he supported President Lyndon Johnson's Great Society programs to help poor people.

George became more interested in civil rights after he took a trip to Vietnam. U.S. troops had been fighting in the Vietnam War (1957–1975) since 1964. George saw black U.S. soldiers bravely fighting and dying for their country. He wanted to help them gain more rights at home. In 1968, he voted for the Fair Housing Act. This law helped people of all races to rent and buy homes in more neighborhoods.

George (RIGHT) loads bags of rice onto a truck during his visit to Vietnam.

In 1971, President Richard Nixon appointed George to a new job. He became the U.S. ambassador (representative) to the United Nations (UN). Within this group, countries work together to solve world problems. George had no experience with foreign leaders. But he got along with people easily.

George and Barbara moved to New York City for George's work. There they met people from around the world. George learned how the United Nations works. He thought the UN did good work in areas of farming, the environment, and health. But he thought it sometimes had little power to solve other world problems.

President Richard Nixon (FAR RIGHT) watches as George (SECOND FROM RIGHT) is sworn in as ambassador.

George prepares to give a CIA report to a Senate committee.

Meanwhile, George began thinking about being president one day. He took jobs that would help him get to the White House. In 1976, George got one of the most important jobs of his career. He became the director of the Central Intelligence Agency (CIA).

This group finds out about activities in other countries. At times, it uses spies. Every morning, the CIA gives the president a report on world events.

As CIA director, George learned about Communist activity around the world. The United States thought Communist nations such as the Soviet Union might take over other countries. (From 1922 to 1991, the Soviet Union included Russia and many nearby nations.)

THE COLD WAR

After World War II, the United States and the
Soviet Union were the world's most powerful
countries. Each feared the other would attack with
nuclear weapons. They had different ideas about
government. The United States was afraid Soviet
Communism would spread to other countries. The
Soviets feared the spread of U.S. democracy. But
they never attacked each other. For more than forty
years, they waged a war known as the Cold War.

In the CIA, George also learned about
military movements and terrorist activity.
Terrorists use violence to create fear and
cause political change.

George learned why the United States
gathers information about other countries—to
protect and serve its citizens. He was amazed
at the bravery of CIA agents. Many secretly
risk their lives to keep the United States safe.

3 A LOYAL VICE PRESIDENT

B y 1979, George felt he was ready to be president. On May 1, he began his campaign. But Ronald Reagan wanted to be president too. He had been California's governor for eight years.

George makes a speech at a 1979 rally. He wanted to be the Republican presidential candidate.

One group of Republicans wanted Reagan. They felt that he shared their conservative Christian values.

In 1979, many people did not know much about George. George believed in God and traditional families. He spoke to voters about his beliefs. But he was a poor speaker. His sentences seemed to have no beginning or end. Reagan was once a movie actor. He was a wonderful speaker.

Republicans chose Reagan as their presidential candidate. George was disappointed. But Reagan chose him as his running mate. Together they won the election. On January 20, 1981, George became vice president.

George enjoyed his work in the White House and weekly luncheons with Reagan. They shared ideas. They laughed at the same jokes. They both liked Mexican food. George wanted Reagan to be a successful president.

REAGAN IS SHOT!

On March 30, 1981, George came close to suddenly becoming president. John Hinckley Jr. shot President Reagan, trying to kill him. While Reagan recovered from surgery, George took care of things at the White House. But he did things quietly, without ceremony. He didn't want people to think he was trying to take Reagan's place as president.

George waves as he boards a plane in Geneva, Switzerland. He traveled all around the world as vice president.

Reagan wanted to end the Cold War between the United States and the Soviet Union. But Reagan hated Soviet Communism. Under Soviet Communism, people could not own land, run businesses, or practice freedom of religion or speech.

George often helped Reagan by traveling to other countries. George met with foreign leaders. He worked to gain their trust and friendship. In March 1985, George met Mikhail Gorbachev, the leader of the Soviet Union. George's meeting helped build a friendlier relationship with the Soviets.

At times, George did not agree with Reagan's decisions. George knew the United States made secret deals with other countries. He knew that presidents sometimes have to take risks. But George worried about some of Reagan's actions. They might hurt George's chances of becoming president one day. One of these actions ended in a scandal called the Iran-Contra Affair.

President Reagan (SEATED) speaks to reporters about problems in Central America in 1985. George (FAR RIGHT) stands in the back with the president's other advisers.

Reagan seemed to have approved a deal with Iran. In 1985, the United States secretly sold missiles to Iran for $30 million. In exchange, Reagan wanted Iran to help free seven American hostages. Iranian terrorists were holding them in Lebanon.

Meanwhile, the United States hoped to spread democracy in Central America. Reagan wanted to help the "contras." These rebels worked against Communism in the country of Nicaragua. For years, the CIA had secretly given contra rebels money, training, and weapons.

Nicaraguan contras cheer and raise their guns at a training camp.

George knew the CIA was secretly fighting Communism. But George did not know everything about what Reagan's aides were doing. By this time, it was against U.S. laws to help the contras. Some aides were breaking those laws. They used money from the Iran weapons sale to help the contras.

It's not clear if Reagan knew about this. But George worried when Congress looked into the matter. The hearings were shown on television. George claimed he did not know about the contra deal.

George still hoped to follow Reagan as president. He still had many friends. By 1986, he and Barbara had sent out 30,000 Christmas cards! George was counting on his friends to help him become president.

4 PRESIDENT BUSH

George served as vice president for eight years. During that time, he never disagreed with Reagan in public. Because of that, many people thought Bush had no vision of his own for the country. But the Republican party supported George. On August 18, 1988, George became their candidate for president. He chose Senator James Danforth Quayle as his vice-presidential running mate.

Crowds listen to George speak at a campaign rally in Medina, Ohio, in 1988.

George ran a fierce campaign against Michael Dukakis, the Democratic candidate. George spoke about patriotism. He believed public schools should encourage children to say the Pledge of Allegiance. But Dukakis didn't think it should be a law. As governor of Massachusetts, he had vetoed (refused to sign) a bill. It would have made teachers lead their classes in saying the pledge.

George told voters he would be tough on criminals. Dukakis had supported a Massachusetts program that let criminals leave prison for the weekend. George made sure voters knew this. And George promised not to raise taxes. Many voters liked this idea.

George won the election. He became the forty-first president. He was inaugurated on January 20, 1989. When George gave his inauguration speech, he thought of the problems ahead. The Democrats controlled Congress at that time. George wanted Republicans and Democrats in Congress to work together. He said, "The American people await action. They didn't send us here to bicker."

WHITE HOUSE FUN

The Bush family enjoyed the White House. The day after George's inauguration, the Bushes opened the White House to the public. George's mother sat in a wheelchair on the lawn, shaking people's hands. George often kept his dogs in the Oval Office. The fourteen Bush grandchildren enjoyed the Children's Garden. Their names, footprints, and handprints are set in bronze in the flagstones.

George visits a classroom in Philadelphia, Pennsylvania. He spoke to students about the dangers of illegal drugs.

Three weeks later, George spoke to Congress. He said he wanted to be the "Education President." George was concerned about the nation's schools. "Some of our students actually have trouble locating America on a map of the world," he reported.

George knew that more money alone could not make schools better. Teachers, parents, and children should work harder. He told parents, "Check on the homework, go to the school, meet the teachers. . . . It's not only your child's future on the line, it's America's."

Americans argued for months about whether people should be allowed to burn the flag in protest. This man, like George, wanted to protect the flag.

He also felt strongly about protecting the flag. He thought no one should be allowed to burn it in protest. He wanted to create an amendment to the Constitution to protect the flag. But Congress did not allow the amendment to become a law.

Like Reagan, George also wanted to end the fear of nuclear war with the Soviet Union. On December 2, 1989, George met with Mikhail Gorbachev again. He liked Gorbachev. George felt he could trust him.

George surprised Gorbachev with plain, honest talk. He told Gorbachev he knew the Soviet system was not working. In some of the Soviet republics, people were beginning to reject Communism. They wanted more freedom and better living conditions. The Soviets could not make enough goods to feed, clothe, and house all their people.

George said the United States wanted to help. The two leaders left the meeting feeling the Cold War was ending. Both wanted their two countries to begin trade agreements.

George Bush and Mikhail Gorbachev shake hands at a 1989 press conference.

As president, George kept building friendships with foreign leaders. He called them just to chat. He shared ideas about world events. He wanted other countries to know the United States cared about them.

George felt proud to be president. He thought working in the Oval Office was a great honor. Every morning, George studied the CIA report. In 1990, he kept a close eye on the Middle East. Trouble was brewing there.

5 DESERT STORM

O n August 2, 1990, the Middle Eastern
country of Iraq invaded its neighbor
Kuwait. The United States and other United
Nations countries were angry. Iraq was a
UN member, and it had attacked another
UN country. George didn't trust Saddam
Hussein, the leader of Iraq.

Saddam Hussein (LEFT) wanted control over Kuwait's oil wells.

George knew he must get Hussein's troops out of Kuwait. Both Iraq and Kuwait are rich in oil. If Iraq took over Kuwait, Hussein would control a large part of the world's oil. He could also invade Saudi Arabia, the world's greatest oil producer.

George feared what Hussein would do with money from huge oil sales. He might attack other countries. Or he might build nuclear weapons.

George wanted to protect Kuwait and Saudi Arabia. He knew how the United Nations could help. He counted on his friendships with world leaders.

The king of Saudi Arabia agreed to Bush's plan, called Operation Desert Shield. King Fahd would allow 250,000 American troops into Saudi Arabia. They would keep out Iraqi forces.

The United Nations agreed to help. Twenty-eight countries came together with military forces in the Persian Gulf region, an area near Kuwait. This show of force worked. Hussein did not attack Saudi Arabia. But he kept his troops in Kuwait. The U.S.-led troops would have to force Hussein's army out of Kuwait.

George (CENTER) and Barbara (LEFT) visit the Saudi Arabian desert in November 1990.

George did not like sending Americans into battle. He knew many could be injured or killed. But he felt military action was needed. On January 16, 1991, the war called Operation Desert Storm started. Air strikes destroyed military targets in Iraq.

On February 24, the ground war began. UN forces attacked the Iraqi army. Tanks stormed across the desert. The battles ended a few days later, on February 28. Iraqi troops finally withdrew from Kuwait.

Some people thought Bush should have ordered troops to remove Saddam Hussein from power. But George would not do this. The UN had agreed for troops only to free Kuwait.

George (AT DESK) makes a telephone call to the leader of Great Britain during Operation Desert Storm.

During the Middle East troubles, George also struggled with issues in the United States. The government was spending too much money. George had to raise taxes. Many people were angry that he had broken his promise of "no new taxes."

Also during the Iraq crisis, George watched the Soviet Union fall apart. Then on December 25, 1991, Mikhail Gorbachev resigned as the Soviet leader. The Soviet Union no longer existed. Instead there were fifteen countries, including Russia.

SUPREME COURT CHANGES

During George's presidency, two of the nine Supreme Court Justices retired. George replaced them with David Souter and Clarence Thomas. Thomas, an African American, came from a poor family and had worked hard to become a judge. George said Thomas was a "model for all Americans."

George (BACK RIGHT) competed with Bill Clinton (LEFT) and Ross Perot (CENTER) in the 1992 presidential election.

The world was changing. And Bush was handling foreign affairs well. But by the 1992 presidential election, many Americans were worried about jobs, health care, and taxes. They wanted a new leader. George lost the election to Bill Clinton.

On January 20, 1993, George took his last walk around the White House. In the Oval Office, he left a note for the new president. He told Clinton he would be rooting for him. Then George and Barbara boarded the presidential helicopter. It made a farewell circle around the White House. George and Barbara were sad to be leaving. They returned to Texas. A new home was waiting for them there.

George had spent most of his life serving his country. He had worked to make the world safer. He encouraged all Americans to love and serve their country too.

When he was inaugurated as president, George shared his vision for the United States. He told Americans to teach children "what it means to be a loyal friend." He also challenged everyone to be "a citizen who leaves his home, his neighborhood, and town better than he found it." George strongly believed in these ideas. They had guided his own life!

TIMELINE

GEORGE H. W. BUSH
WAS BORN ON
JUNE 12, 1924.

In the year...

1942   George joined the United States Navy and became a pilot.

1945   he married Barbara Pierce.   Age 20

1948   he graduated from Yale University.

1951   he and John Overbey founded an oil development company in Midland, Texas.

1966   George was elected to the U.S. House of Representatives.   Age 42

1971   he was named U.S. ambassador to the United Nations.

1976   he became director of the Central Intelligence Agency.   Age 51

1981   he became the vice president of the United States.

1985   he met with Soviet Union leader Mikhail Gorbachev for the first time.

1989   George became the forty-first U.S. president.   Age 65

1990   he nominated David Souter to the Supreme Court.
George sent U.S. troops to defend Saudi Arabia after Iraqi forces invaded Kuwait.

1991   he ordered Operation Desert Storm.
he nominated Clarence Thomas to the Supreme Court.

1992   George lost the presidential election to Bill Clinton.

2001   he saw his son George W. Bush inaugurated as the forty-third U.S. president.

2005   George and former president Clinton helped raise money for Hurricane Katrina victims.   Age 81

STILL SERVING

After George left the White House, he still wanted to serve his country. He and Barbara helped raise money for cancer research. George also teamed up with former president Bill Clinton to help others. When disasters struck, they raised money for victims. In 2004, they helped after a tsunami destroyed coastal towns in Southeast Asia. In 2005, Hurricane Katrina struck the Gulf coast of the United States. George Bush and Bill Clinton toured the flooded areas to show their support.

George and Barbara also raised money for the George Bush Presidential Library and Museum. It is located on the campus of Texas A&M University. It holds 39 million important historical documents and 60,000 objects. These include an Avenger plane like the one George flew in World War II.

Bill Clinton (LEFT) and George (RIGHT) visit children whose homes were destroyed by the 2004 tsunami.

FURTHER READING

Davis, Kenneth C. *Don't Know Much About the Presidents.* New York: HarperCollins Children's Books, 2003. This fun book has a question and answer format.

Donovan, Sandy. *Running for Office: A Look at Political Campaigns.* Minneapolis: Lerner Publications, 2004. Learn how presidential candidates raise money and reach voters through TV commercials, rallies, mailings, and other ways.

Hamilton, John. *The CIA.* Edina, MN: Abdo Publishing Company, 2007. This book explains how the CIA works and includes a timeline and fun facts.

Streissguth, Tom. *Russia.* Minneapolis: Lerner Publications, 2008. In this book, you will learn about the land and people of Russia.

WEBSITES

George Bush Presidential Library and Museum: Interactive Learning Programs
http://bushlibrary.tamu.edu/education/programs.php
Learn about holidays in the White House and design your own room at the White House.

U.S. Presidential Pets: Then and Now
http://kids.nationalgeographic.com/Stories/AnimalsNature/Uspresidentialpets This site gives fun facts about the pets and other interesting animals at the White House.

US Presidents—George H.W. Bush
http://www.whitehouse.gov/kids/presidents/georgehwbush.html This page includes some personal information about Bush, with links to other biographies.

Select Bibliography

Alfonsi, Christian. *Circle in the Sand: Why We Went Back to Iraq*. New York: Doubleday, 2006.

Andrew, Christopher. *For the President's Eyes Only: Secret Intelligence and the American Presidency from Washington to Bush*. New York: HarperCollins Publishers, 1995.

Beschloss, Michael R. "George Bush 1989–1993." In Robert A. Wilson, ed. *Character Above All: Ten Presidents from FDR to George Bush*. New York: Simon & Schuster, 1995.

Bush, George. *All the Best, George Bush: My Life in Letters and Other Writings*. New York: A Lisa Drew Book/Scribner, 1999.

Bush, George, and Brent Scowcroft. *A World Transformed*. New York: Alfred A. Knopf, 1998.

Catherwood, Christopher. *A Brief History of the Middle East*. New York: Carroll & Graf Publishers, 2006.

Hyams, Joe. *Flight of the Avenger: George Bush at War*. San Diego: Harcourt Brace Jovanonich Publishers, 1991.

McGrath, Jim, ed. *Heartbeat: George Bush in His Own Words*. New York: A Lisa Drew Book/Scribner, 2001.

Parmet, Herbert S. *George Bush: The Life of a Lone Star Yankee*. New Brunswick, NJ: Transaction Publishers, 2001.

Reed, Thomas C. *At the Abyss: An Insider's History of the Cold War*. New York: Ballantine Books, 2004.

INDEX

Acknowledgments

For photographs and artwork: © Rex Features USA, p. 4; George Bush Presidential Library, pp. 7, 11, 12, 15, 16, 18, 19, 24, 31, 39, 40; National Archives (i080-G-16871), p. 9; AP Photo, pp. 10, 21; © CORBIS, p. 13; © Shel Henshorn/Hulton Archive/Getty Images, p. 17; © Ron Sachs/Corbic NY/CNP/CORBIS, p. 20; © Cynthia Johnson/Time Life Pictures/Getty Images, p. 26; © Diana Walker/Time & Life Pictures/Getty Images, pp. 27, 33; © Cindy Karp/ Time & Life Pictures/Getty Images, p. 28; © Terry Ashe/ Time & Life Pictures/Getty Images, p. 34; © Dirck Halstead/Time & Life Pictures/ Getty Images, p. 35; © Mike Nelson/Getty Images, p. 38; AP Photo/Doug Mills, p. 42; AP Photo/Gerald Herbert, p. 45.

Front Cover: George Bush Presidential Library;
Back Cover: Terry Ashe/Time & Life Pictures/Getty Images.

For quoted material: pp. 32, 43, George Bush's Inaugural Address, January 20, 1989, http://www.presidency.ucsb.edu/ws/print.php?pid=16610; p. 33 (all), George Bush's Address on Administration Goals Before a Joint Session of Congress, February 9, 1989, http://www.presidency.ucsb.edu/ws/print.php?pid=16660; p. 41, Lane Crothers and Nancy S. Lind, *Presidents From Reagan Through Clinton, 1981–2001: Debating the Issues in Pro and Con Primary Documents,* Westport, CT: Greenwood Press, 2002, 143.